My Journey from Berlin to Newport Beach

My Journey from Berlin to Newport Beach

How a Teenage Immigrant Achieved the American Dream

Rudy Mariman

with Craig Batley

Published by
Hybrid Global Publishing
301 E 57th Street, 4th fl
New York, NY 10022

Copyright © 2018 by Rudy Mariman and Craig Batley

All rights reserved. No part of this book may be reproduced or transmitted in any form or by in any means, electronic or mechanical, including photocopying, recording, or by any information storage and retrieval system, without the written permission of the Publisher, except where permitted by law.

Manufactured in the United States of America, or in the United Kingdom when distributed elsewhere.

Mariman, Rudy
My Journey from Berlin to Newport Beach:
How a Teenage Immigrant Achieved the American Dream
LCCN: 2018965152
ISBN: 978-1-948181-37-2

Cover design by: Cynthia Lay / www.speakerwebsites.com
Cover photo: Craig Batley
Copyediting: Ayse Yilmaz
Interior design: Medlar Publishing Solutions Pvt Ltd., India
Photo credits: Rudy Mariman, John Bloom, Bradford Portraits
Permission credits: University of Portland

www.mariman.com

CONTENTS

Illustrations   *vii*
Preface   *ix*

CHAPTER 1
Berlin Germany   1
The Early Years

CHAPTER 2
Immigration to America   9
A New World

CHAPTER 3
My Stepfather George and the Farm   15
Living on the Farm in Oregon

CHAPTER 4
High School & College   23
The Formidable Years

CHAPTER 5
Employment *Engineering*   31
*Success is where preparation and **opportunity** meet.*

CHAPTER 6
Learning the Land Business 33
Second Job

CHAPTER 7
Saving Money 39
"A penny saved is a penny earned"—Benjamin Franklin

CHAPTER 8
Apartment Career 43
There is nothing permanent except change. What's dangerous is not to evolve.

CHAPTER 9
Influential People 49
Mentors, Role Models, and Influencers

CHAPTER 10
Reflections, Lessons Learned & Random Thoughts 59
Every day, I set aside time for thinking.

Afterword 67
Acknowledgements 71
Epilogue 75

APPENDIX
Rudyisms 77
Others' Favorite Quotes 83
Exhibits 85

ILLUSTRATIONS

Rudy's grandfather in 1940	2
Grandfather's delicatessen store in 1951	4
Rudy age 5, in Berlin 1946	5
My mom at 20 years old in 1934	7
November 6, 1954 in Tempelhof Airport	9
Leaving on honeymoon	13
Rudy County Fair Grand Championship Angus Bull	17
Rudy First Car, 1949 Oldsmobile	25
17 years old in 1958	26
Visiting Grandfather in 1969	50
George and Heidi Mariman in 1955	52
Rudy Mariman at the Mariman & Co. corporate offices in 2018	89

PREFACE

If you are reading this book, chances are you are a recipient of a scholarship from the Rudy & Gloria First Generation Scholarship Program. Mr. Mariman shares his journey of leaving his country of origin, Germany, arriving in Estacada, Oregon, via New York with one pair of corduroy knickerbocker pants, two shirts, a sweater, and a jacket in his wardrobe. Today, Mr. Mariman is a multimillionaire living in Newport Beach, California. Learn how Mr. Mariman achieved success in business via hard work, successfully graduated from the University of Portland with a Mechanical Engineering Degree, was offered a high paying engineering job, worked a second job, lived below his means, saved his money, and invested in southern California residential apartments.

I met Rudy Mariman 45 years ago. We were both living at the Oakwood Garden apartments, now known as the Eight80, directly across from Newport Harbor High School. We met on the tennis courts and agreed to play a set of tennis. Afterwards, Rudy invited me to his two-bedroom apartment and shared with me the opportunity to buy land in Antelope Valley. I declined to buy but we agreed to meet at his office to discuss the possibility for me assisting him in selling land west of Lancaster, California. Rudy had been saving money since he began earning money on his stepfather's farm in Estacada, Oregon, when he first arrived from Berlin in America at age 14, speaking limited English. It turns out Rudy was a prodigious saver, a habit most successful people develop at an early age.

This book is a story about a first-generation German kid arriving in America, the land of opportunity, with only two shirts, a pair of corduroy knickerbocker pants, a sweater, and a jacket. He shares his journey of navigating the transition of leaving his homeland, coming to a foreign country, entering school with limited English skills, working on his stepfather's farm, graduating from high school and college, and securing a high paying engineering job in Southern California. Rudy has lived the American dream.

As you read these pages, think about the obstacles and challenges Rudy faced and what shaped his early teenage years, instilling in him the desire to succeed and thrive in his adopted country, the USA. Perhaps you, too, have faced some of the same experiences. Rudy learned the value of hard work while living on the farm. He realized attending and graduating from a university was an important step to future opportunity.

Rudy's experience may not be typical, but farm life provided him the opportunity to work and earn money. Rudy's stepfather expected him to work and undertake the chores demanded of farm life. There wasn't much to distract young Rudy in the mid-1950s: the portable transistor radio had just been released to the stores, color TV was a rarity, and movies were seldom viewed. Of course, there were no cell phones, tablets, computers, email, Facebook, Instagram, Twitter, or any internet to intrude on a teenager's time.

In sharing his story, Rudy's desire is to inspire today's teenaged first-generation immigrants living in America to succeed, sometimes, against all odds. If Rudy can overcome the challenges of moving to a foreign country, working hard, studying while in school, listening to encouraging mentors, and taking advantage of opportunities when they arose, then you too can be successful.

If you have a desire to excel and live up to your potential, then follow Rudy's example. Shortly after WWII, a teenaged boy from Berlin, Germany, with his mother, left their home, their friends and family, and sailed to America. Traveling from New York to Portland, Oregon, mother and son began an incredible journey eventually leading both to Newport Beach, California. After graduating from the University of Portland with a Bachelor's of Science in engineering, Rudy worked at an aerospace company while selling land in Antelope Valley, California, and eventually embarked on a career of owning and managing apartment buildings in Orange and the surrounding counties.

Four decades later, Rudy has amassed a large apartment building portfolio valued in the multimillions. He now has earmarked his fortune to the University of Portland, to benefit first generation immigrant young adults attending his alma mater. Scholarship money is now available to first-generation immigrant students, helping them reach their academic potential, including the possibility of future financial success.

Rudy's story exemplifies how a first-generation student, after becoming a citizen of the USA, persistently pursuing opportunities, and focusing on a career you love, can achieve success in the land of opportunity. As a recipient of scholarship money from The Rudy & Gloria Mariman First Generation Scholarship Program, this book is here to help you learn the lesson that someone in your situation can find great success. Yes, the career and business possibilities are waiting for your commitment and energy to pursue success for yourself and for those you care about. Rudy is an American success story, and his story can show you how you too, can be a success story.

As you embark on your college career, you might ask yourself 3 questions while reading this book. First, what valuable life lesson(s) did you learn while reading the book? Second, what lesson are you going to apply in your own life going forward? Lastly, what plan of action will you implement to improve your own life?

CHAPTER 1

BERLIN GERMANY

The Early Years

At the end of World War II on September 2nd, 1945, conditions in Berlin, Germany were terrible. Much of the city devastation resulted in vast piles of rubble. Prior to the war, much of the population lived in large, multi-story apartment blocks. Some 600,000 apartments were destroyed. Only 2.8 million of the city's original population of 4.3 million still lived in the city. Many were killed in the Allied bombing. Most of the missing people had fled the city.

There were severe food shortages. Water mains and sewage systems were destroyed. Disease was rampant and sewage everywhere. The stench was terrible. Rail links with the countryside and rest of Germany were destroyed. Those who survived had no way of making a living. Factories were destroyed. Shops were closed because goods were unavailable. Food was the most immediate problem, but housing, because of all the destruction, was also a huge problem. Life in the city became never-ending hunger, disease, housing shortages, unemployment, and abject poverty. The Allies hired mostly women to begin to clear away the rubble. But even among the rubble, children were seen playing in the ruins. The situation became even worse as the first post-War winter approached. Families could live in damaged homes during the summer. During the winter however, living in homes with holes in the walls, and without coal, was a different matter.

I was about eight years old living in Berlin, when my mom received a telegram from my father, Franz Kalbas, who was living in Vienna, and reassuring us everything was going to be fine. My mom and I traveled via train to Vienna, which was a major ordeal, because back in those days, Russians surrounded Berlin. We could have traveled by air, but it was too expensive.

I remember my grandfather stuffing some money in a liverwurst sausage he gave us for the trip. The East German police came to the station outside of Berlin and entered our train car to search passengers. They looked at the sausage, where my mom's entire life savings were hidden inside.

Rudy's grandfather in 1940.

The two East German police officers looked at each other and said, "What should we do with this sausage?" The officer banged it against his forearm while looking at my mom, who was struggling to not look alarmed, knowing all her money was in there. Thinking it was a plain old sausage one of the policemen declared, "Let's just leave the sausage here. What are we going to do with it?" I can remember the look of relief on my mom's face.

My father met us at the Vienna train station. This was the very first time I remember seeing my father. Previously, I never knew him. He was a military officer in the German army, and during WWII, he was stationed away from my mom and me. After he met up with us, he temporarily placed us in a boarding house with about 50 to 60 beds. We stayed there for several weeks. The living conditions, being communal, were obviously challenging to say the least. There were no showers. My mom and I went to the public bath house, paid an entrance fee, and after my mom had taken her bath, I used the same water and tub for my bath. Temporarily, mom enrolled me in the local school.

After the first week or so, my father's brother visited us and desired to tell my mom the truth about my father, who lived on the outskirts of Vienna, in Linz. He escorted mom to where my father was living so she could witness what her husband was up to. They took the train to the outskirts of town where my father's 4th floor apartment was located, knocked on the door, and a woman opened the door. He said, "I am Franz's brother, and this is his wife." My mom explained she was there to see Franz, my father, but before he came out, the woman said she had 3 boys from a prior marriage and a fourth boy would be too many. "I don't need another boy to raise". However, if I had been a girl, she would probably welcome her to the household. She had assumed that the purpose of the visit was to pawn me off to my father, which of course, was the last thing on my mom's mind.

Of course, the shock of my father having another family was overwhelming for my mom. When my father finally came to the door you can imagine the pandemonium that ensued; it was a fiasco. Fortunately, I was not present when all this took place. After the visit, my mom was most distraught to learn her husband had abandoned his wife for another woman. My uncle liked my mom and wanted her to know the truth. Even so, mom was determined to save her marriage and desperately tried to coax her husband to reunite with us. Mom got a job and attempted to save her marriage. Her first job was attending to two Doberman dogs owned by a neighboring family, but she could not control the dogs on walks. Later she became a caregiver to an old man, and we moved into his house. I can remember waking up in the night and hearing the gentleman peeing into a night pan, a sound I will never forget. My mom attempted to mend fences with my father for almost a year, to no avail. Reuniting as a family was not to be.

My grandfather (Opa), Albert Wiedeman, mom's father, was always the anchor in our little family. My grandfather coaxed my mom back to Berlin, in 1949. He said he had good news for us. We flew back to Berlin, whereupon my grandfather informed us he repurchased the little grocery store he had previously owned prior

Grandfather's delicatessen store in 1951.

to WWII, including living quarters in the back. I vividly remember milk being delivered to the store at 2:00AM in big metal canisters, because of the noise it created awakened me. My mom worked in the store with her mother and father. The store provided income and a place for my mom and me to live. I vividly remember my mom telling me she had managed to bring home all the savings my grandfather stuffed in the sausage when we left Berlin. Her life's savings were intact. Looking back, my mom instilled in me the importance of saving money, but more importantly, to keep your savings growing.

Prior to evacuating Berlin to the countryside, I was enrolled in the local school beginning in first grade. (On the first day of school, the custom was to bring a gift for the teacher). When we left the city, I was in third grade and did not attend school for about one year. However, shortly after arriving back in Berlin, my mom enrolled me in a school for fifth, sixth, & seventh grades. As I remember, the school was three, maybe four stories tall, and was an all-boys school. It took me 20 minutes to walk to school. Homework was assigned up the wazoo! Discipline was evident in the classroom. When the teacher walked into the classroom, there was to be immediate silence. Student conduct in the classroom showed total respect for the teacher. Class schedule included Saturdays, from 8am to 1pm.

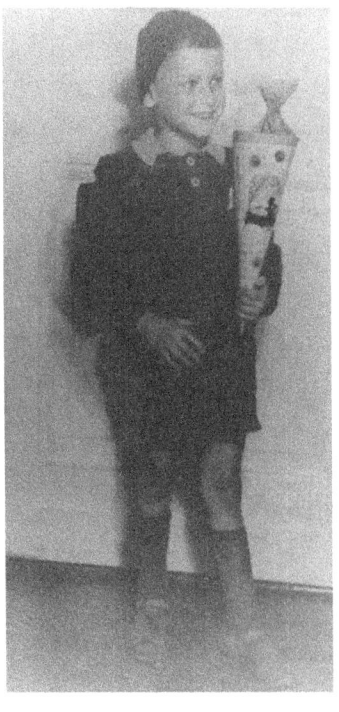

Rudy age 5, in Berlin 1946.

The school curriculum had 3 career pathways. Testing occurred during sixth grade, and depending on your scholastic standing, you had three career paths to choose from: the practical path (trade), the technical path (engineer/science), or the PHD path (doctor/lawyer). I qualified for the technical path. The school day began at 8:00AM and ended at 3PM. The curriculum consisted of class in the mornings, with lab & testing in the afternoon, six days a week.

A homeroom was assigned to all students, along with a home room teacher. My classmates and I stayed all year in the homeroom classroom, with teachers specializing in various subjects visiting every hour throughout the school day. Each teacher had maybe two or three books for the whole class, which were shared among 35 students. Typically, two students were assigned a few chapters in the book for homework, learned the subject matter, and then were required to share for 20 minutes what they learned in front of the class, answering student questions. Participatory student learning was standard classroom practice. The teacher would grade our presentation, including how we answered the questions asked by the rest of the class.

School days were long. We had plenty of assigned daily homework. I woke up around 6:30AM, readied myself for school, walking each morning about 20 minutes with all the other students, to school. It was a privilege to own a bike, but bikes were scarce. My friends and I never owned a bike. I don't remember many of my fellow students riding a bike to school, either.

After school I often played soccer in the streets or in a vacant lot cleared of the war rubble. There were no organized school sports' programs. When not playing soccer, I would occasionally be asked to help in the store after school, as well.

Usually, on Sunday afternoon my grandfather would take us to the Spree River on the outskirts of the city in his little second-hand

Adler car. At the river there was entertainment, dancing, and music. During the summer, my grandfather treated us to coffee cake and a nice lunch. During the winter months, I traveled with a couple of buddies, via the subway, to go sledding or ice skating on skates fastened to our shoes. Christmas was a big event in Germany. We exchanged presents on Christmas Eve. I received one present from my mom and one from my grandfather.

During the beginning of my eighth grade year in school (I was 13, almost 14 years old), my mom became friends with a store customer who was excited about immigrating to the state of Oregon, in the USA. The family had two children, and promised to correspond after arriving in Oregon. Upon their arrival, this family met a gentleman named Frank Carmody, who worked for the railroad, and had an interest in marrying a German woman. Neither Frank Carmody nor my mom could speak each other's language, so a young 18-year-old girl, a customer at the store, transcribed my mom's letters from German to English, for Frank Carmody and vise versa. My mom corresponded with Frank, exchanging letters and pictures for about six to nine months, culminating in a long-distance marriage proposal. Frank sponsored our immigration to America, to Portland, Oregon.

My mom at 20 years old in 1934.

The decision to leave her native Germany, was not an easy decision for my mom. In fact, she nearly decided against leaving Berlin. Quite frankly, she agonized over whether she should travel to a strange country with only her son. The uncertainty caused her to break out with a case of shingles, which compounded the situation. When mom's case of nerves subsided, her shingles began to heal. Soon after, my grandfather shared with my mom that he had an opportunity to immigrate to Nebraska in the late 1930's before World War II began. A school chum of his sent him a ticket, but he got cold feet and didn't go. He chose to stay in Berlin, a decision he always regretted. He strongly encouraged my mom to immigrate to Oregon and start a new life. He said, "do it for Rudy".

It was a big decision to move from the comfort of the store and adjacent living quarters. Our apartment consisted of a private one and a half bedroom with shared toilet (you brought your own soap and toilet paper), wash basin, small kitchen, and living area. Again, like in Vienna, we had no bathing facilities at the store. We would go to a bathhouse once a week that had eight private baths, where my mom would bathe, and then I would take my turn, and again, use the same bath water. It was a daunting and bold decision, moving to an unfamiliar foreign country, speaking no English. Moving to America, the land of opportunity, changed my life.

CHAPTER 2

IMMIGRATION TO AMERICA

A New World

The day finally arrived to leave Germany. My grandfather took me aside and said to me, "As you embark on your journey to America, you are now old enough to look after your mom." I realized at that moment a new awareness of responsibility. In 1954, we flew from Berlin to Bremerhaven to circumvent the Russian zone surrounding Berlin. Shortly after arriving, in Bremerhaven, we boarded the SS America and sailed to South Hampton, England, then departed on the nine-day ocean voyage to New York. The seas were stormy, and most passengers like my mom and I were berthed in the lower decks in third class, where many passengers were seasick. Fortunately, I met a boy about my age who was traveling first class in

November 6, 1954 in Tempelhof Airport.

a stateroom close to the promenade deck. He took me to the upper deck where the wind was fierce, maybe 30 knots, almost blowing me down, but the refreshingly cold, sea salt air gave me respite from my seasickness. I was amazed to experience how my new-found traveler friend's family could live and eat in first class. I didn't realize it at the time but visiting first class on the SS America left quite an impression on me.

We landed in New York harbor on November 21st, 1954, which coincidently, happened to be my grandfather's birthday. I remember observing my new friend climbing in a Cadillac with his family on his way home. My mom and I stayed overnight at a modest hotel and the next day boarded a train for the three-day transcontinental trip to Portland, Oregon. I really don't remember too much about the train ride other than it was long. Upon arrival in Portland, we were greeted by my mom's Berlin friends and her sponsor, Frank Carmody, possibly my future stepfather and mom's potential husband. As you recall, Frank and my mom previously had corresponded and exchanged pictures via a young girl translating. I remember my simultaneously exciting and awkward feeling meeting Frank for the first time. Mom said, "Remember Rudy, I don't have to marry him." I was immediately relieved and said to myself, "well that is pretty good, since my initial impression of my mom's suitor was unfavorable". It turns out Frank liked my mom much more than she liked him. Imagine the adjustments required of my mom meeting her suitor for the first time, needing a place to call home, and perhaps a job—a tall order to say the least.

Frank was elated meeting my mom, and suggested we meet his parents on the way to his home. I was nearly 14 years old, spoke very little English, and my mom spoke no English. Even though I don't remember much, I recall feeling most uncomfortable. I can still remember how awkward it was meeting Frank's parents for the first time. It is something you'll never forget. Frank proudly introduced us to his parents, who liked us right away.

Frank then drove us to his house. I don't remember much other than he had three cars, one for himself, one for my mom, and one for myself, even though I wasn't of age yet. Frank had been planning for months in anticipation of meeting who he considered to be his future wife. He really wanted to make this union successful.

Frank, it turned out, had two previous childless marriages. Marrying mom would have been his third marriage. He had a nice little house for all of us and figured his new German frau would be able to cook and clean for the house. He most definitely expected an amorous relationship with his mail-order bride. My mom had other ideas.

It would have been inappropriate to stay at Frank's house, so we stayed at the home of my mom's Berlin friends: a little two-bedroom, one-bath rental home. Later, I moved into my mom's friend's aunt's house. She had two boys close to my age. I vividly remember these two brothers were generous and giving, something I was not used to. I didn't grow up in a sharing environment, having no brothers or sisters. I remember Rick, who was maybe a year older, showing me his closet with 25 shirts and 20 Khaki pants, quite a contrast to the one pair of corduroy Knickerbocker pants, two shirts, a sweater, and jacket in my wardrobe. Rick said, "Here Rudy, you are welcome to wear anything in my closet." I was just beside myself.

I remember Ted was 16, I think Rick was 15. I soon learned these boys had access to one of their parents' cars, which was unheard of back home in Berlin. In fact, most families in Berlin did not own a car. Imagine me cruising around in a car with my new-found friends sitting in the front seat and a cute girl sitting in the backseat. It was surreal.

During our interim living accommodations, my mom decided to enroll me in the local Portland public high school. I found myself ahead of the students in my class, since I had already taken algebra I & II, geometry, and trigonometry. Case in point, when the teacher wrote equations on the blackboard for homework, I knew the answers and completed the work before leaving the class.

Rick and Ted's mother mentioned to her parents, the Rehbeins, who lived in Estacada, Oregon that my mom and I had just arrived from Germany and suggested they host a little dinner party. Saturday night was agreed upon. George Mariman expressed an interest in meeting the recent arrival from Berlin, my mom. The Rehbeins agreed to invite George Mariman to introduce him to my mom, "the lady from Germany." Being twice married, George was cautiously interested in meeting mom. The dinner party invitees included Herr and Frau Rehbein, my mom, me, and George Mariman.

At the dinner table, there was a moment where no one wanted to begin eating, so my mom subtly pointed a finger at George urging him to begin eating as a guest of honor. Afterward, George immediately was attracted to my mom.

After the dinner party, Frank was totally sidelined, since my mom was never really attracted to him as a potential husband. My mom always felt a little bit awkward ignoring Frank, since he sponsored us to immigrate to Oregon, but as a suitor, it was not to be.

George liked mom's conservative dress appearance. She wore new flat soled shoes from Germany and a rather plain dress. After dinner, George asked mom if she would be interested in working as his housekeeper. The arrangement lasted for about a week, cooking and cleaning at George's house. Looking back on it, George had certain ulterior motives, but initially my mom was not receptive to any personal relationship.

At the end of the week, her bags were packed when George came home from the mill. She said to him, "You know, I don't think this is the kind of work for me, please take me back to the home of Irma Kaplick, my girlfriend in Portland." George obliged and drove my mom back to Portland. However, the next day, my mom happened to forget her German English dictionary at George's house. The next day, George asked if it was alright to return the dictionary and visit my mom. During that visit George invited mom to a spaghetti and meatballs dinner in Portland. In 1955, going out to dinner was a big deal.

Leaving on honeymoon.

The romance between George and my mom lasted about two months: before and after Christmas, during the holiday season. George proposed marriage. The original Berlin couple, who immigrated to Portland, Oregon witnessed the marriage just 50 days after mom and I arrived in America. George and Mom were married on January 9th, 1955.

CHAPTER 3

MY STEPFATHER GEORGE AND THE FARM

Living on the Farm in Oregon

We moved into George's house in Estacada, Oregon in mid-January, 1955. The farmhouse was a three-bedroom, one-bath house. I had my own bedroom. I had never dreamt that I would ever be living in a big farm house in a bedroom I could call my own. Just a few short months earlier, I was living in a cramped little, one and half bedroom apartment behind a grocery store in Berlin, boarding a ship sailing the Atlantic Ocean to New York, arriving via train to Portland, Oregon, and then temporarily sharing a small two-bedroom house with the Kaplick family and their kids, Hans and Renate. Moving into my stepfather's spacious country farm house, with my own bedroom, was a drastic change. The rapid contrast from my tiny apartment in Berlin, sharing a two-bedroom home in Portland, to an Estacada farm house, was hard to fathom.

George was a first-generation Belgium immigrant arriving in America when he was 18 years old, together with his two brothers and a sister, via Canada. One of George's first jobs upon arriving in Portland was working in a large sawmill, guiding logs in the pond to the circular saw. It was a dangerous job, requiring skill and knowledge, moving desirable logs in a position to be cut. Depending on the market demand for lumber, George would choose which logs were to be harvested. During the winter months, the pond water was cold; it was often raining, and logs were slippery. His job description required him to walk on logs in the pond and maneuver them to the conveyor belt to be cut to order. While standing on the logs, he occasionally fell into the pond. It was a tough job. Like many immigrants, he was very grateful his parents had the courage and stamina to immigrate to the USA. Thus, for eight years George mailed the majority of his income to his parents until he was 26 years old.

You would think there would be a dog or cat on the farm, but no, George had no pets on the farm, only a herd of Black Angus cattle. There were about 28 head of cattle and one bull. Raising cattle was a for-profit business for George. He would slaughter several steers each winter, with new calves being born in the spring. George had no chickens, goats, or pigs on the farm either. However, we had a large garden which my mom cared for, planting vegetables, including some fruit trees. My mom transitioned from being a city dweller to a farm wife. She started really liking the task of harvesting fresh vegetables from the garden. And George was just elated, since his previous wife had no interest in gardening.

Each day of the week, I had farm chores to complete. I also helped Mom with household chores when needed. When it came to cleaning dishes, Mom would wash the dishes, and time permitting, I would dry the dishes. Mom spent a lot of time in the kitchen, cooking, canning, and cleaning. She was the first to arise in the morning and begin preparing breakfast. George usually arrived in the kitchen for breakfast first, and then Mom called me to come downstairs and join George for breakfast. High school class hours were nine to three. I had chores before and after school, and generally on the weekends. After getting dressed in the morning, and before school, I would often feed the cattle.

As I remember, mom kept me kind of isolated and sheltered. Occasionally, George would say, "Uh, you know, that boy of yours is so spoiled, he stinks." The relationship I had with my stepfather, George, is best described as boss/employee. George was the guy I reported to for work. George never filled the role of being my dad. I respected George, but I relied on my Mom, who always wanted the best for me.

There was a barn not far from the house where some of the farm equipment was stored, and the Black Angus cattle were fed and sheltered during the winter.

During the fall and winter months, we would fatten the cattle, giving them grain and molasses. During the summer months, we would let the cattle graze in the pasture.

I was a member of the local 4H club. The club had an annual "Biggest Bull" contest, which I entered with a bull George allowed me to feed and prepare for the contest. I was awarded first place in the 1957 4H bull contest.

I had various other jobs, including barn and barnyard manure

Rudy County Fair Grand Championship Angus Bull.

clean up. Also, George instructed me how to cut the large-sized area of grass surrounding the house and barn with a power lawnmower. I mowed grass every week during the summer and as needed during the winter.

George had a total of 180 acres when he married Mom, doubling the farm acreage in later years. Mom approved and supported George's business dealings.

I worked on George's farm during my three years as a sophomore, junior, and senior, while attending school. George and the crew would cut down trees on the farm, then we hauled them to George's portable saw mill. The cut timber would leave the field littered with stumps, which we would dynamite. On the weekends, work consisted of clearing land, picking roots, picking rocks, and throwing them on the flatbed trailer being towed by the tractor. Sometimes there would be one, two, sometimes three other kids my age helping. Occasionally, I would be driving the tractor, a much easier task than walking behind the trailer picking up roots and rocks and loading the flatbed trailer. The trailer was hinged, enabling us to back onto the side of a hill and dump the load.

After clearing the land, we would till the soil and plant Alfalfa grass seed. Towards the end of summer, the combine tractor would cut the alfalfa, while baling the hay, dropping each bale onto the field.

George paid us 50 cents an hour for the weekend farm work. This was my first paying job, and it felt great. Just the aspect of receiving money on a weekly basis was a wonderful feeling. The idea of getting paid for work felt good. I was on George's payroll.

George, and his brother Frank, owned the portable sawmill where we hauled the logs from the farm. Being portable enabled George and his brother to set up the mill operation close to the timber source. I worked at the sawmill every summer during my high school and college years. George employed maybe seven or eight mill employees. The sawmill company would set up their operation at various locations, depending on where there was sufficient timber to be harvested. George and his brother Frank, owned the mill, but later George bought out Frank's interest.

The summers during high school would mostly consist of working at the sawmill. We would leave the house a little before seven and worked from 8:00 till 5:00PM. Mom would always pack our lunch in lunch boxes. George drove his pick-up the one-hour ride to work each day, picking up Henry Crocker, the mill foreman who lived a few miles down the road. George had a contract with the railroad to supply thousands of railroad ties. Railroad ties were six by eight inches, and eight feet long. We would be home between 6:30PM to 7:00PM for dinner, depending how long George would stop at the tavern on the way home.

During my second summer in 1956, the mill's edgerman job became available. The job consisted of tracking and monitoring logs to be cut into rough lumber, eventually, trimming and plaining the rough lumber into finished lumber of various sizes. I was making a $1.25 an hour, stacking lumber the previous summer, but now with my new job, I got a pay raise of 50 cents per hour, making $1.75 an hour. Just the idea of working for higher wages was terrific. I saved nearly all my earnings.

As mentioned, often after work at the mill, George would stop at a little tavern about halfway home. George was very outgoing. He was a man's man, everyone loved him. He projected an aurora of being authentic. He had a gift socializing with people. I admired George for what he represented, a working man with strong values. Depending on who was patronizing the tavern, George would enjoy conversing with his friends or other customers, sometimes staying for a few hours. If I suggested we should go home early, he paid no attention, and I had to just hang out until George was ready to head home for a late dinner prepared by my mom.

My poor mom had no idea when George might arrive at home. However, you could always rest assured that on Wednesday nights, he'd be home right at 6:00PM. Why? Because that was Fight Night. Boxing was televised every Wednesday night, and he wasn't about to miss a boxing match. In his early twenties, George was an amateur boxer, and thus, he never missed watching a televised fight.

Occasionally on the nights we'd arrive home at midnight, George would be drunk, and we would eat a warmed up, premade dinner prepared by Mom. Wives and husbands had different relationships in the 1950s. My mom did the cooking, cleaning, planting, tending, and cultivating the garden and overseeing the general farm responsibilities, while George worked at the mill.

George liked to go hunting and fishing. During hunting season, he would love to hunt deer and elk in eastern Oregon. George asked my mom to accompany him a few times, but he preferred to take a couple of his hunting buddies (so did my mom). George owned a camper which fit on the bed of his truck. George and his friends would stay the weekend.

George, being a hunter, owned several rifles, shotguns, and a few hand guns. Occasionally, George and I would shoot guns while in the woods. I never went hunting with George, nor did I enjoy fishing in the lake. George had a little boat, which he'd put on top of the camper. George invited me fishing several times, but I didn't like handling the slimy trout. To this day, I do not consider myself a fisherman, that's for sure. My mom went fishing with George on several occasions. She later confided to me, she grew to enjoy fishing.

Immigrating from Germany to the USA, settling in Oregon, and living on George's farm during high school was a good transition for me. The work ethic of farm life gave me a solid frame of reference while adjusting to my new environment. The fact that George paid me for most of the farm work and gave me a job at the saw mill was instrumental in learning and understanding the work-reward relationship, resulting in me earning a paycheck. I also appreciated the value of being paid according to one's skill and experience. Farm life was good.

CHAPTER 4

HIGH SCHOOL & COLLEGE

The Formidable Years

After George and Mom married, they enrolled me in the Estacada high school. Initially, the school principal was going to enroll me as a freshman, but after my interview, the principal decided I should enter school as a sophomore. School had commenced the previous September. I enrolled mid-year in high school on January 15th, 1955, the year Elvis Presley released his hit record, *I Don't Care if the Sun Don't Shine*. It was a major, major culture shock to me. One thing I remember, all the girls seemed to be attracted to the jocks, the boys on the football, basketball, and baseball teams. My impression was the teachers favored the athletes, as well.

The contrast of Oregon public schools with my Berlin schooling was stark. In Berlin, we had a homeroom class and the homeroom teacher stayed with us throughout high school. The homeroom teacher would teach two or three courses and the other six or seven courses would be taught by different teachers, who would come visit our classroom. We were assigned the same desk in the same classroom for all 4 years of high school. There were no student lockers in the hallways. Instead, we had our own personal desks. Oregon public schools had one class in homeroom, and the students moved from classroom to classroom for each subject. Student lockers were located in the hallways.

Not being conversant in English was a major obstacle. Initially, I struggled with adjusting to school life. Total immersion into the school curriculum with limited English was a real challenge. Soon, however, my English improved. Looking back, total immersion was the best way to learn English and understand class instruction. At first, I didn't really have any friends, and was a bit self-conscious and overwhelmed. I felt out of place and uncomfortable with the school social scene. I never went to the Prom. I seldom attended the sporting events after school, either. I was a bit shy and felt very isolated during the school day. Rather than engage with students, I would generally go to the next class and just sit there by myself before and in-between class. Kids were hollering and laughing and having a good old time in the hallway. I would go to class sometimes 20 minutes before the first class began. I do not have fond memories of my high school years. All through high school, I had few real friends. I suffered from lack of self-esteem. In Germany, such a condition is referred to as *Minderwertigkeits Komplexe*, defined as a person that doesn't think very much of himself—a horrible way to go through life.

It probably didn't help that I had a very protective mom. I remember having one friend over to the house, and my mom made it so miserable for him, he left after 10 minutes and never came back. And from then on, I never had one kid come to my house. Unlike many of my high school classmates, I worked almost every day on the farm, all the while saving my money.

I always liked cars. One of the high points of my high school experience was buying a car with my summer earnings. I bought my first car on my 16th birthday, December 16th, 1956. I bought a 49-year

High School & College

Rudy First Car, 1949 Oldsmobile.

Oldsmobile for $600 cash. Not many students, especially 16-year-olds, owned a car let alone paid for the car with money saved from two years of working on the farm and at the sawmill. I kept the Oldsmobile until the last year in college, when I traded it in for a black, red interior, stick shift, square rear-windowed, '57 Volkswagen Beetle.

Most of my classmates turned out for sports after school. I turned out for football for a short while but soon discovered I knew little about the game. It was nothing like playing street soccer in Berlin. I really did not enjoy being a bench warmer, watching everybody else play. As already stated, high school was not exactly a wonderful, nor memorable time of my life.

A milestone of my high school days was becoming a U.S. citizen. Like most foreign-born immigrants, we all have to apply for USA citizenship. I remember studying for the citizenship test. I took my test in Portland, Oregon and participated with dozens of other immigrants in the naturalization ceremony. I became a U.S. citizen on May 4th, 1958.

Mom and I discussed going to college during my high school years. She reminded me that my biological Father had an electrical engineering college degree. I remember my mom started pleading with George to consider paying for my college education. George's comeback was, "I don't know why I should pay for Rudy's college when my three kids from my previous marriage didn't go to college." After much discussion, George finally came around and he said, "OK, here's what I'll do. I will pay half of Rudy's college tuition for the first two years and after that he's on his own." The fact George was willing to pay for half of my college tuition for the first two years of college meant a lot to me. I want to stress the fact, when somebody believes in you and is willing to support your college expenses, it gave me confidence to succeed in my college career. George's decision to pay for half of my college tuition was a huge morale booster for me. Midway through my senior high school year, I started to gradually improve my self-esteem. Working on the farm, and earning grades, qualifying for the honor roll, enabled me to begin the process of seeking success for myself. As you know, my stepfather and I, did not have a father-son relationship, but I did respect him as a businessman and as an employer. He was always fair. It felt good that George believed in me and was willing to partially subsidize my college expenses. In the 1950s, most high school students did not go to college.

17 years old in 1958.

Having saved my summer earnings, I was able to pay the college tuition not covered by George. George's belief in me and my mom's encouragement together, provided me the motivation to apply for acceptance to the University of Portland. Every kid needs to have parents or a teacher who encourage them to consider going to college. If I did not have the support of family, I may not have gone to college. Fortunately, I made the decision to attend college and was accepted into the engineering program. I had a natural affinity for math and science, and excelled in these high school courses.

I recollect George being somewhat tenuous about my college career, maybe wondering if I would even graduate. During my junior year in college, George realized I was determined to complete my engineering degree. It occurred to George that I might be the first child of his who obtained a college degree. Prior to that time, he would sheepishly introduce me as his stepson. He gradually changed his tune and began to introduce me as a "college man." During my junior year in college, when I was with George and his buddies, George would brag, and stated, "My boy here, he is a college man". Sometimes he would share with his friends, "Are you aware that my boy is a college man?" This is the first time that George referred to me as, "his boy", rather than stepson. It felt good. He was proud to have his stepson attending college. George's change of attitude made me feel more like family. Mom was especially pleased.

When you are 17, you are not sure what to declare as a college major. Perhaps because my birth father was an engineer, I chose engineering as a field of study. Math came relatively easy to me. The engineering curriculum was challenging, to say the least. If a student did not have a background or proclivity for math or statistics, it was a struggle. Fortunately, I was not one of the 50% who would drop out of the program before graduation. I mean, the engineering curriculum was brutal. With all the homework, and especially the labs, your weekends were shot.

I graduated from high school in 1958 and four years later, I graduated from college in 1962. Fortunately, in the early 1960s, graduate engineers were in huge demand and I easily landed a job. Job recruiters from all over the United States came to the University, resulting in 13 job offers for me, and many job offers for my fellow graduating engineers. It was a challenge deciding which job offer to accept. Recruiters representing companies from coast-to-coast were selling the merits of working for their company. I could've accepted a job anywhere in the country. I vividly remember the Douglas Missile & Space System (referred hereafter as Douglas), division recruiter painting a beautiful picture of Santa Monica, describing the beach parties, California girls, Hollywood, and Beverly Hills. I decided I didn't care how much salary Douglas was offering, I was going to accept a job with them. I accepted the Douglas' offer of $555 per month, the second-highest offer behind Boeing's offer of $565.

Upon graduation on May 27th, 1962 from the University of Portland, I drove to Southern California in my Volkswagen, leaving Oregon and traveling to Santa Monica. I put two big boxes of books in the back seat with all my clothes piled on top of my books. I didn't know anybody in Southern California, but I had a job waiting for me. It took me two days to arrive in Santa Monica, traveling through 100-degree Fresno, through the Bakersfield Valley, having no air conditioning in my Volkswagen. Crossing the Santa Monica Mountains, coming across the grapevine, leaving the San Fernando Valley, into the LA basin, the temperature dropped to about 75 degrees.

Like so many immigrants before us, my mom and I sailed the Atlantic Ocean on an ocean liner 3,419 miles to New York. Then we endured a 2,364-mile train ride to Portland, Oregon. My mom and I traveled a total of 5,783 miles for the opportunity to start a new life. Without really knowing it, I was in the midst of living the American dream. It was tough on my mom leaving home, but like she used to say, "We all survive." Thanks to my mom's desire for a better life for me, I was starting a new job in Southern California at the Douglas Missile & Space System Division in Santa Monica.

The journey of immigrating to America from Germany, living and working on the farm, immersing myself in Estacada high school, graduating from University of Portland with an engineering degree, and landing a high paying engineering job in southern California, was life changing. I was scheduled to report for work on June 8th, 1962.

CHAPTER 5

EMPLOYMENT *ENGINEERING*

*Success is where preparation and **opportunity** meet.*

I secured an interim motel room for six dollars a night until I could locate more permanent accommodations. I was super anxious to see the ocean. I unpacked my stuff, jumped back into the car, proceeded to Ocean Boulevard, traveling west. Arriving at Santa Monica beach, I viewed the beautiful, blue Pacific Ocean in sunny California. Seeing those beautiful palm trees lining the boulevard, I proceeded to travel north on Ocean Boulevard and saw a sign pointing towards Beverly Hills. Then traveling east down Santa Monica Blvd., I turned left on Beverly Boulevard, and I noticed cars like Mercedes, Cadillacs, and Lincoln Continentals passing me by. A little further up the street, both sides were lined with mansion-sized houses. I had only seen such homes on TV. I still remember the feeling of awe when I drove by these huge houses.

I reported for work at Douglas the morning of June 8th, 1962 and met a few engineers in my work group. After staying at the Lanai motel apartments a few days, I knew I couldn't afford first and last month's rent to secure an apartment. I decided to find an apartment, and room with one of my fellow engineers. Within a day or two, I put a little ad on the bulletin board at work hoping to find roommates willing to share an apartment. A fellow employee and I rented a one-bedroom apartment for $150 per month, or $75 each.

A few months later, three of my fellow engineers and I secured a four-bedroom house paying only $200 per month, or $50 a month each. All of us were unmarried and had a party every other Friday night. We had wonderful times.

Douglas was awarded the GAM-87 SkyBolt program in February 1960, two years prior to my employment, with initial deployment projected in 1964. The GAM-87 SkyBolt project was an air-launched ballistic missile that was designed to be carried on the B-52H bomber. I worked six months on this project at the Douglas's Missile & Space System division. Then just prior to Christmas, the government cancelled the GAM-87 SkyBolt project, and I received a pink slip. Douglas proceeded to lay off nearly 4,000 engineers, including me, in December of 1962, a short six months after being hired. I realized no job is safe, even an engineering job.

Being laid off was certainly an eye opener for me. Being unemployed was probably a good thing, since it set the stage for me to realize there is no job guaranteed. I proceeded to prepare my resume, seeking a new job. Since engineering jobs were in demand, a short time later, I secured a new job in January 1963 at the Mobile Oil Company in Torrance. I was one of eight engineers working at the Mobile Oil facility but decided to go back to aerospace engineering one year later. I took a job at North American Aviation, in Downey, and subsequently transferred to the City of Commerce and worked there until mid-1965.

Finally, Douglas, rehired me in 1965, two and a half years after being laid off, and I worked another four years until 1969 when I decided to end my engineering career. After seven years, I left the engineering profession, two weeks after we put two men on the moon on August 1969. I had been working in the land sales business part-time and decided to make land sales my full-time job.

CHAPTER 6

LEARNING THE LAND BUSINESS

Second Job

My land business began as a part-time second job while working at Douglas. In 1964, I purchased a two and a half acre parcel in Antelope Valley, making monthly payments for several months. You get busy with life and tend to just keep making those monthly payments. During the 1960s, real estate law allowed a land company to purchase, say, one hundred sixty acres, and split it four ways into four 40-acre parcels. Subsequently, the company then again split the 40-acre parcels into ten-acre plots, and finally, the tens are split into two and a half acre parcels. Thus, the 160-acre parcel is divided into 64 two and a half acre parcels. The land companies purchased a 160-acre parcel at wholesale, and then sold the 64 two and a half acre parcels retail. In the 1960s, using this method, a property owner was able to avoid the subdivision map act. Later, in the late 1970s, the map act was amended prohibiting such practices.

My first land purchase was priced at retail. I paid $6,500 (retail) for my two and a half acres, 10% down payment, payable at $50 a month, making 180 payments over 15 years, including six percent interest. Buying land at retail prices leaves little room for future appreciation. About four months after my land purchase, I decided to investigate the Antelope Valley real estate market and revisit my property. I talked to local real estate brokers and basically concluded I had paid too much for my acreage. I discovered my land purchase was going to be a long-term, NOT a short-term investment. I was not interested in a long-term investment proposition. Consequently, I executed a deed in lieu of default, giving the property back to the land company. Many investors viewed their investment as a 10 year or 15-year ownership commitment. I was looking for a much shorter-term investment. So, I educated myself on how the land business was structured, talked to several more Antelope Valley brokers and became familiar with the business of buying and selling acreage.

After being laid off by Douglas, I decided I needed to have a second source of income. I was determined to become a buyer and seller of land while working full time as an engineer. I was not satisfied being in the boom or bust aerospace industry where you were making good money, and because the government cancels a project you find yourself unemployed. I found myself having lunch with my fellow engineers, sometimes waiting for a new government contract and they would tell me: "You worry too much. This has been going on for years and years and is going to continue going on for years and years." I took that statement to mean, I would be laid off and unemployed again in the future. This was not acceptable to me. Dear readers, always have a contingency plan. My plan was to have a second job enabling me to save all the money I earned in the land business.

The aerospace boom-bust scenario did not sit well with me. I asked myself: "What if, what if, what if, I couldn't readily find another job or maybe would have to move to another state?" I began to research the sales component of the land business by answering ads in the LA Times to purchase land. I would fill out a coupon requesting information to purchase land, and the company would send out a salesman to sell me a two and a half acre parcel. Over a period of six months or so, I talked to eight or ten salesmen, but never bought anything. I was "going to school" by listening to the salesman's sales pitch. All the salesman wanted to sell me two and a half acre parcels. Listening to the salesman's dialog helped me a great deal.

After the tenth salesman, I met Paul Connor in 1965. He was a good-looking man. He looked like Yule Brenner, but bald headed, and twice my age. After about an hour of visiting with me, we developed a report. He invited me the following week, on Saturday morning, to play volleyball with his friends. I told him I was not interested in buying a two and a half acre parcel, so he pitched me to become a finder, or "bird dog", of potential buyers. I decided to work part-time for Paul. Instead of talking about trivia at the office coffee machine, I began to ask some of the engineers if they ever thought about making extra money. If the answer was yes, I would set an appointment to meet Paul Connor, who would share how to make money by investing in land.

I set appointments with maybe three, four, five, up to six engineers, sometimes after work at 5:30PM, at a nearby restaurant to meet Paul Connor. Paul would make his presentation about investing in land, and invariably half of the engineers signed up to look at Antelope Valley land the following weekend. If Paul sold land to one of the engineers, or to family members, I would earn a 10% commission of the sale, payable 50% in cash and the remainder monthly, over a period of three years. Paul was a salesman's salesman, a man's man, and very likable.

I worked with Paul for two, maybe three years. Over that time, Paul closed about ten sales, and I collected my ten percent finder's fee. A typical sale was $10,000, and I was paid $1,000: 25% to 50% cash

($250/$500) and the balance ($500–$750) paid in residual monthly installments of $25/month. Remember, my paycheck each month was about $555, sometimes more with overtime, and now I was collecting a total of $1,000 in finders' fees from Paul Connor, upon a sales closing. I had been saving more than half of my paycheck, with a few thousand dollars in the bank, and now was banking every two or three months another $500–$750 cash by referring potential buyers to Paul Connor.

During this time, I concluded the best way to enter the business was to buy larger 20 or 40-acre parcels, splitting them, then selling the remaining five or ten-acre parcels. I had a monthly payment to make on the 20 or 40-acre land parcels. After splitting the land four ways and selling each parcel, I created four monthly payments which created net positive cashflow. Looking back, I was always motivated to have more cash savings in the bank.

To anyone reading this book, take note: having cash savings in the bank, enabled me to buy a 20 or 40 acre, or sometimes an 80-acre parcel on favorable terms, usually with 10% cash down, making payments for 15 years on the balance, and thereby putting myself in the land business. Instead of giving Paul prospective land buyers, I began selling prospects five and ten-acre parcels at about the same price land companies were selling two and a half-acre parcels. So, you see, my sales pitch advantage to the buyer was he received twice as much acreage from me compared to the prices large land companies were charging their customers.

I gradually stopped working for Paul Connor and went into business for myself, part-time while working at Douglas. I was buying acreage wholesale and selling it semi-retail, but still half price per acre compared to, say Occidental Petroleum, with a large subdivision consisting of 6,500 acres with a little lake and club house, including plans for a golf course (which was never built). I had a list of their two and a half sales prices and proceeded to sell my parcels for less than half price per acre compared to Occidental Petroleum. Remember, I was working full-time at Douglas, and going to USC night school, where I was enrolled in two night classes: one began at 3:30PM to 6:30PM, and my second class began at 7:00PM and ended at 10:00PM. I earned a Master of Science Systems Management. If you want to get ahead, you must keep your options open. I was motivated to succeed in business. Soon I had created $100,000 in land contract receivables, paying out $1,000 per month, payable for 15 years. After seven years working full-time as an engineer, I decided to quit my job and started selling land full-time, using a team of Douglas engineers as "finders" for prospective land buyers willing to invest in Antelope Valley land.

I was 32 years old and living in Huntington beach. I decided to move into the Oakwood Garden Apartments (now known as Eight 80 Apartment Homes) located across the street from Newport Harbor high school, in Newport Beach. I found waterfront office space and began to sell land from my office, instead of my apartment. I hired a real estate agent, Craig, who eventually set three evening appointments for me, four nights a week. We mutually benefited from the arduous schedule of meeting three prospects per night, I trained Craig how to cold call, and he set the appointments. By 1974, together with my cohort, Craig, I created over $1,000,000 of land contract receivables.

CHAPTER 7

SAVING MONEY

"A penny saved is a penny earned"
—Benjamin Franklin

1955 First job working on the farm. Beginning wage was approximately 50 cents an hour, later received $1.25 per hour. I saved most of my earnings.

1956 Job promotion during summers working at the sawmill at a wage that began at $1.25, and later raised to the job of edgerman at $1.75 per hour.

1956 On my 16th birthday, I paid $600 cash for 1949 Oldsmobile with partial savings I accumulated since 1955.

1962 First job after college graduation at Douglas, starting salary of $555/mo.

1962 A fellow employee and I rented a one-bedroom apartment for $150 per month, or $75 each, later moved to a $200 four-bedroom house split four ways or only $50 per month.

1964 **Second Job** land sales commissions. A typical sale was $10,000 and I was paid $1,000: 25% cash and the balance paid in residual monthly installments. Remember my paycheck each month as about $555 and now I was collecting a total of

$1,000 sometimes $2,000 in finders' fees from Paul Connor every month. I had been saving more than half of my paycheck, had a few thousand dollars in the bank and now was banking another $500–$750 cash, referring potential buyers to Paul.

1969 **Land Sales.** Having cash in the bank, I decided to go into the land business myself and began buying 20–40 acre parcels, and sometimes 80-acre parcels on terms. I split these parcels to five and ten acre parcels for resale. Please note, I purchased land on terms, and subsequently sold land on terms. I never paid more than 10% down, and the land owner would take back a first trust deed payable over 15 years.

Leverage is key, preserving cash. I would split these tracts of land four ways, and instead of giving Paul Connor prospective land buyers, I began selling prospects five and ten-acre parcels at about the same price land companies were selling two and a half acre parcels.

1972 **Live below your means**. Moved to Newport Beach into a $250 apartment. I saved 90% of my income, a little extreme, but I always had cash savings. Possessing cash allowed me to take advantage of real estate investment opportunities.

1972 **Savings, the key to Financial Success. Saving is the key to Prosperity.** In the previous ten years, I managed to save $300,000, primarily collected from monthly land payment receivables.

1973 **Own your own Home.** I bought my first home, where I have lived for 45 years. I paid $285,000, using the principle of leverage. Ideally, everyone is able to own the home in which they live. I chose to purchase my home with leverage. My down payment was only $18,000. The terms were: $200,000, assumed first mortgage, $50,000 owner financed second mortgage with $35,000 down payment, with the broker carrying a third mortgage of $17,000, leaving me with only $18,000 cash invested. The value of the home has increased more than 20-fold.

1975 **Own Apartments/Income property.** Purchased my first apartment building, consisting of 43 units at a price of $15,000 per unit in Costa Mesa, which I still own, now worth $400,000 per unit.

1976 **Discounted note.** I bought an $80K second trust deed note for $50K, at 34% discount and saved $30K.

1976 **Refinance.** I refinanced my first trust deed note on the 43-unit apartment building, paid off the $50K and put $100K in bank.

2018 **Only Buy–Seldom Sell.** The last 43 years, my company has acquired and manages almost 2,500 units in Southern California.

When beginning your career, I want to stress the importance of building cash savings. Don't take things for granted. I think it's prudent to go through life asking, "What if? What if, I get laid off? What if an attractive investment opportunity comes to your attention?" In my case, working a second job enabled me to save, and eventually, invest in land and later in apartments. Without my savings, I would not have been able to invest, and today, I would not own hundreds of apartment units. I pursued having some fun on the weekends, but I balanced leisure time with (it turns out mostly) work time. I worked many weekends on my second job. I never took things for granted. My weekends were really devoted to my second job, which eventually became my new full-time self-employment. Saving at least 10%

(I saved in excess of 75%) of your earnings is essential for financial success.

Also, a key to financial independence is avoiding personal debt, like credit cards, postponing payments with no interest financing, student loans, pay day loans, auto loans. A real estate mortgage is debt secured on appreciating assets and I do not consider it to be "personal debt".

CHAPTER 8

APARTMENT CAREER

*There is nothing permanent except change.
What's dangerous is not to evolve.*

My longtime friend, Bill Bokovoy, is an engineer by trade, but transitioned into owning and managing a 32-unit apartment building. He micro-managed his property and consequently, he was able to cash flow his property very nicely. Bill extolled the benefits of owning apartments over the years, but I was not interested. However, all that changed when Craig and I attended a weekend course on how to fix up income property and rent or sell it. Craig said, "You should buy income property." When I began looking for a building to purchase, I realized I needed to find an experienced real estate broker who could educate me and help me buy apartments.

I received a tip from a broker who knew of 43 units located in Costa Mesa, all two bedroom, one and a half bath units which may be for sale. He did not want to represent me, he only wanted a referral fee if I purchased the property. I agreed to his terms. I called the seller and determined the owner might be a legitimate seller. I contacted my broker, Bill Rietsch, and he put the transaction together. Even though I had purchased many land deals, I knew nothing about purchasing apartment buildings or income-producing property.

Recognizing that I'd never purchased an apartment building, I needed to rely on an experienced broker who knew how to get the job done. I just didn't have enough knowledge. I was embarking on a totally new kind of real estate investment, namely income property. It is important to emphasize the importance of recognizing what you don't know and surround yourself with at least one person whom you respect and has the skillset to close the sale. I interviewed several brokers and selected Bill Rietsch to be my broker. Bill was actively selling apartment buildings to investors, so I had a lot of confidence in him. The arrangement with Bill was, "I will pay you three percent commission, but you must take your commission on a note and trust deed recorded on the property, payable interest only, monthly, until I refinance or sell the property." He agreed to my terms. He had other income coming in and was OK with the arrangement.

I paid $620,000, obtained a $465,000 loan (75%), the owner carried back a $80,000 second, and Bill carried his commission of $18,600 in a third trust deed. My down payment was $56,400 only 9% of the sale price. I want to emphasize the leverage aspect of this transaction. To top it off, the seller called me up six months later and stated, "I hate to bother you, but I am getting a divorce, and would you be interested in paying off his $80,000 note at a discount?" I said, "Let me get back with you tomorrow." I offered $50,000, a discount of 37.5%. My banker lent me the $50,000, and I saved $30,000.

I then proceeded to do some minor rehab, raised the rents and contacted the Savings & Loan, who made the original first trust deed loan, to see if they would refinance the loan. The appraised value of the property had increased sufficiently, enabling me to qualify for a new loan, paying off the existing first, second, and the third (broker commission) trust deeds. To top it all, off the refinance generated cash proceeds of $100,000, which gave me back the $50,000 cash buy out of the second, and most of my original down payment. I said to myself, "This is the kind of business that I want to pursue". The year was 1976, and 42 years later, I am still in the apartment business, a business I thoroughly enjoy. I had several opportunities to sell this property at a nice profit, but never sold. I own this 43-unit building today, all these years later. By the way, this apartment building has increased in value nearly 30 times the original purchase price.

Over the years I have managed my properties in-house. Years ago, I hired Ruth McClure to help me with managing the properties. She had a lot of property management experience and stayed with me for 15 years. She oversaw the onsite property managers and maintenance staff. I did not visit the properties much, and my newly hired quasi-regional manager did not visit the properties much either. (I later discovered this was a mistake). She oversaw my eight property locations. To help her, I decided to hire an independent property management company. However, I was unable to track my expenses before decisions were made, which made me uncomfortable. It turned out, hiring an independent property management company did not work for me. I was more of a hands-on manager, always emphasizing buying properties with leverage, preserving my cash. During those years, I was allowing deferred maintenance to accumulate, and the management company wanted authorization to spend more money than I was willing to allocate. Maybe I was too hands on, micro-managing. For me, it was the dilemma of balancing my cash with maintenance expense. I wanted to conserve my cash to expand the portfolio. I was always very reluctant inputting any kind of money into the properties. I suppose I was at fault for this policy, and years later realized it was much better to allow no deferred maintenance, keeping the properties in pristine condition.

In the year 1995, I purchased 101-unit building in Garden Grove, using extreme leverage. This property was built in 1988. Peter Hauser, a broker I had not used before, called me and said, "I know you're looking for leverage properties. I think I've got one for you." The terms of the purchase resulted in $300,000 down payment, I "assumed" an existing 10-year construction loan, that was due in 3 years, in the amount of $6,500,000. The purchase price was $6,800,000. I purchased the building for $300,000 down, by taking subject to the existing first trust deed loan without the lender's approval, a risky proposition. The lender soon contacted me and demanded I pay an additional $1,000,000 down. The lender threatened to call the loan, even though we were making the loan payment as agreed. The lender began to send nasty letters wanting me to pay down the loan. The lender was concerned the property was over encumbered. I asked Craig to help negotiate with the bank to extend the due date on the loan. Craig wrote letters to the bank explaining that we were raising the rents and the loan payments would remain current. The bank correspondence continued for about 18 months until I had enough cash flow on the property to justify qualifying for a new loan to pay off the construction loan. The bank did not want to foreclose, so they allowed me to continue making payments, keeping the loan current. And that's what we did. The terms of this purchase enabled me to leverage into a $6,800,000 apartment building property for a mere $300,000 down payment. This type of transaction is seldom possible. When I purchased this property, it had negative cash flow. I was able to fine tune the management to a point where I could bring the property to a break-even status in approximately 18 months. I have owned this property for almost 25 years.

I found myself getting too involved in the decision making as to which vendors to choose, when I did not have a clue what vendor to use. I realized that, just perhaps, I might need to hire independent professional expertise. A big turning point occurred when I met with property managers, Rich & Rick Hoegler, at one of my properties, 14 years ago. Rich made me realize I was not maintaining my properties to maximize long-term ownership. He was right. I allowed deferred maintenance to accumulate for 30 years. It was time I tackled this problem and change my management philosophy.

Rich said that I needed to rehab this property. I realized I needed to rehab all of my properties. Rich offered to take me on a tour of some properties his company was renovating. We looked at about four properties in the midst of various stages of rehabilitation. One property was completely emptied of tenants and all units were being remodeled, including exteriors and landscaping.

I was sufficiently convinced Rich and Rick had the experience I was looking for and hired them to undertake a 4-year complete renovation of my properties. I discussed my decision to eliminate all deferred maintenance with Craig Batley. Craig had previously mentioned I should consider changing my view of preserving my cash at the detriment of delaying property repairs, such as roof, exterior paint, dry rot, parking lot slurry coating, tree trimming, and more. I spent well over $5,000,000 to complete the project. Diligent focus on attending to all maintenance requests and long-term reinvestment in capital investment in all my properties, became my focus.

In the long run, it pays to keep the properties in pristine condition. When deferred maintenance is not allowed to occur, tenant profile improves, tenant turn over decreases, and cash flow improves. Allowing no deferred maintenance was one of the best property management decisions I ever implemented. I am very happy with making the investment to catch up with property maintenance. I totally changed my investment management philosophy and now do not allow deferred maintenance anymore. Today all of my properties are in pristine condition. The message to any property owner is, "Don't let deferred maintenance pile up on you."

The Mariman & Company apartment portfolio numbers over 2,000 units. We have about 70 employees consisting of managers, assistant managers, leasing agents, and maintenance personnel on site at the various properties. The corporate office has 15 additional seasoned, dedicated employees.

The Company owns properties in approximated 21 Southern California locations, most are in Orange County, a few in LA County, and some in San Diego County. The corporate business plan is to continue to purchase apartment buildings, expanding the portfolio and growing the business.

CHAPTER 9

INFLUENTIAL PEOPLE

Mentors, Role Models, and Influencers

I recommend young people search for role models you can admire, people who take an interest in your career. *A role model is a person whose behavior, example, or success is or can be emulated by others, especially by younger people.* Role models are important because they help guide you in the right direction. As you make life decisions, role models and mentors provide inspiration and support when needed. They provide living examples of how to live a fulfilling, happy life.

A **positive influence** occurs when someone or something **influences**, inspires, or otherwise encourages someone to be a better person or discover one's own potential. Possibility thinking is one of the great keys to success. It takes you beyond positive thinking. While positive thinking helps you correct faulty thinking patterns, possibility thinking helps you to become aware of your hidden possibilities. Possibility thinking helps you to become the person you could be. A positive attitude can really make dreams come true, it did for me. Lou Holtz best describes what is possible when he states: "Ability is what you're capable of doing. Motivation determines what you do. Attitude determines how well you do it."

The following people were the most influential people on my journey to achieving my human potential.

Grandfather (Opa): Albert Wiedemann

My grandfather played a pivotal part in our little family. Everything revolved around him, he was the back bone of our family, since my father was not home much. A classmate of my grandfather went to Nebraska in the 30s and invited him to immigrate with him to the USA. My grandfather had tickets in hand, however, at the last minute, he got cold feet. My Mom also got cold feet at the last minute, but my Grandfather strongly encouraged my mom to immigrate to the US. He would say, "Don't make the same mistake that I did in the 1930s", then he added, "If not for yourself, do it for Rudy."

Visiting Grandfather in 1969.

My grandfather was counsel, guidance, and protector of Mom and I, and was of utmost importance. His decisions were crucial at pivotal life changing events, during WWII, leaving behind his store in Berlin, after WWII, and proved to be central in mom's decision to immigrate. He was the person who told mom to move to the countryside during WWII. After the war, he provided employment and a place to live for Mom at his store. His encouragement for Mom to immigrate to America certainly made him a very instrumental person in my life, second only to my mom.

Mom: Heidi Mariman

Born in 1914, my mother was a typical young German woman growing up in the 1920s and 30s. Raised by my grandfather and grandmother, she was schooled through high school, met my father, Franz Kalbas, when she was 26 years old, married him, and birthed her one and only son, who she named Rudy, in 1940. Germany was a prosperous country, but the Nazis were in power and Germany was in the midst of WWII making it extremely difficult for ordinary citizens. Germany was in a full-blown war economy. My father joined the military shortly after marrying my mother and consequently, was away from home most of the time. I did not know him. I don't remember much about my father. He was conscripted into the German army and seldom home.

To better understand the living conditions of the German citizens during the years between 1938 to 1945, I will review a few historical events. German war expansion began in 1938, with the annexation of Austria, and then continued with the occupation of the Sudetenland and then all of Czechoslovakia in 1939. Both had been accomplished without igniting hostilities with the major powers, and Hitler hoped that his invasion of Poland would likewise be tolerated.

To neutralize the possibility that the USSR would come to Poland's aid, Germany signed a nonaggression pact with the Soviet Union on August 23, 1939. In a secret clause of the agreement, the ideological enemies agreed to divide Poland between them.

Shortly after noon on August 31st, 1939, Hitler ordered hostilities against Poland to begin at 4:45AM the next morning. At 8PM on August 31st, Nazi S.S. troops wearing Polish uniforms, staged a phony invasion of Germany, damaging several minor installations on the German side of the border. They also left behind a handful of dead prisoners in Polish uniforms to serve as further evidence of the supposed Polish invasion, which Nazi propagandists publicized as an unforgivable act of aggression.

Little more than one year before I was born, at 4:45AM, on September 1st, 1939, the invasion began. In Poland, German forces advanced at a dizzying rate. Some 1.5 million German troops invaded Poland all along its approximately 291-mile border. Employing a military strategy known as the blitzkrieg, or "lightning war," armored divisions smashed through enemy lines and isolated segments of the enemy, which were encircled and captured by motorized German infantry while the Panzer tanks rushed forward to repeat the pattern.

On September 28th, 1939 (28-day invasion), the Warsaw garrison finally surrendered to a relentless German siege. That day, Germany and the USSR concluded an agreement outlining their zones of occupation. For the fourth time in its history, Poland was partitioned by its more powerful neighbors.

In June 1941, Hitler attacked the USSR, breaking his nonaggression pact with the Soviet Union, and Germany seized all of Poland.

I was born on December 16th, 1940 during WWII; my father was away at war most of my very early childhood. He never did reunite with my mom after the war. The war ruined the lives of many Germans, especially, the ordinary citizens. Berlin was a dangerous place to be living, so, at my grandfather's insistence, my mom moved with me to the German countryside away from most of the fighting and bombing. We moved back to Berlin at the end of the war in 1945, when I was 5 years old.

George and Heidi Mariman in 1955.

In summary, my mom was the most instrumental and influential person in my life. She protected me during WWII, moving to the German countryside. Later, she made the decision to immigrate to America when I was 14 years old, married George Mariman, and we lived and worked on my stepfather's farm. She also strongly encouraged me to attend college, arranging for George to pay one half of my college tuition for the first two years. My engineering degree enabled me to accept a job in Southern California, the land of opportunity.

George Mariman: My Stepfather
George was a first-generation Belgium immigrant arriving in America when he was 18, along with two brothers and a sister, via Canada. George was born in Belgium, traveled to Canada with his family, with the goal of immigrating to America. George dropped out of school in the fifth grade, but like many mid-century immigrants was self-made, taking advantage of the freedom to become a success through self-determination and hard work. We did not socialize with George's family. Living on the farm was a great place to grow up as a teenager. George was firm but very fair. His work ethic set the tone for life on the farm. I never really thought of George as my father. Our relationship was more employee/boss. I worked for George after school, weekends and during the summers 1955 to 1962. George paid me the going rate, starting at 50 cents per hour, eventually earning $1.75 per hour.

Dick Farley:
He and two partners ran a land company bussing people up to Antelope Valley on weekends on two Greyhound buses. They had up to 100 part-time salesmen. I learned a great deal from Dick. He helped me fine tune my land business by thinking outside the box.

Paul Connor:
Most charismatic guy I ever met. Offered me a part-time job of referring (bird dog) fellow engineers who were interested in investing to buy land in the Antelope Valley.

Within a year I was making more money working part-time for him compared with my full-time engineering job at Douglas Missile & Space System Division. Paul tutored me about the land business showing me how to sell, while helping hone my people skills.

I worked two years for Paul, being paid commission on his land sales. After working approximately two years for Paul. I started my own referral (bird dog) team and mirrored Paul's business model with one major difference—I was selling land I purchased for the purpose of reselling the land to investors interested in owning land in West Antelope Valley.

Craig Batley:
The Oakwood Garden apartments, now known as Eight80 apartments, had three tennis courts and typically anyone would go hang out at the courts and ask if anyone would like to play tennis. I was living at The Oakwood and so was Craig Batley. I met Craig Batley at the courts and challenged him to a set of tennis. Maybe he challenged me, I just don't remember. We played tennis and I remember he was a pretty strong player. I got to know Craig a little bit and invited him over to my apartment with the idea I would pitch him on investing in Antelope Valley land. I showed him my relief map of the valley and before I could finish my sales pitch, Craig informed me that he had purchase a one and a quarter-acre California City parcel when he was 21 years old and backed out for the same reason I did. Long term investment was not for him.

However, we developed a relationship where I hired him to cold call prospective land buyers, making appointments in the evenings to meet me for the purpose of selling five or ten-acre parcels priced at semi-wholesale. I paid Craig the standard 10% of the sale with 50% of the cash down payment (usually 10% of the purchase price) and the balance payable monthly over the next three years. With my coaching, Craig perfected his cold calling skill to the point he was making up to three appointments per night, Monday thru Thursday, beginning at 6:00PM on the hour, ending at 9:00PM. Occasionally, we would make appointments on Saturdays, as well. Together, we generated over a million dollars of land contract receivables. All appointments were made at the office, instead of my apartment. During this time, I suggested we attend a weekend seminar sponsored by Lowry-Nickerson to learn how to buy income property, fix it up, and sell or rent these properties. After taking the class, Craig strongly encouraged me to consider buying income property, primarily residential income units. I wasn't really too keen on the idea, initially.

The seminar showed us the benefits of owning rental property. It took me several months to shift from owning land, to buying apartments. Getting used to a whole new aspect of owning real estate I knew nothing about was a big step, and a whole new aspect of real estate investment. You never know how your career may change, in my case from engineering to land sales, and eventually owning and managing apartments. Be open to change and progress in your career. Since 1973, off and on, Craig has been instrumental in helping me organize and streamline my business.

Bill Rietsch:
My acquisition broker from 1975 to 1995. When I find someone, who can perform the job, I stay the course. A few of my employees have been with me for over 25 years

Peter Hauser:
My acquisition broker from 1995 to present, for the past 23 years.

Richard Hoegler
I hired Richard, of Pan American Properties, Inc., to help me renovate my apartment community portfolio. The goal was to eliminate all deferred maintenance which had accumulated over the years. It was a collaborative effort of sharing knowledge and creative ideas when implementing the rehabilitation process. I employed Richard's son, Rick, to be the oversite manager of the project, who at the beginning of the renovations was new to the renovation process. He matured as the project evolved. I had confidence in Pan American Properties, and it paid off. The experience was invaluable for both of us.

Rick Hoegler
I trusted Rick to undertake the renovation of my multi-family property portfolio. He was new in the business, but I believed in the father and son team. The rehabilitation was a tremendous success. The project lasted four years at a cost of more than five million dollars. Congratulations, Rick, on your promotion to President and owner of Pan American Properties. You proved yourself overseeing my renovation.

Shawn Boyd:
"I really want to stay in the game..." Rudy Mariman said those words to Shawn Boyd at their first lunch meeting in August 2008, and thus, began a journey, that as of this writing, has lasted ten years and resulted in the acquisition of more than 300 million dollars of real estate. Shortly after that first meeting, they'd chart a course re-shaping Mariman & Co. to become one of California's most prolific direct investors in affordable housing. Shawn understood and presented

affordable housing in a way that Rudy hadn't considered before. Putting their trust in each other, they strategically and methodically, shifted from a very local investment profile to become a statewide powerhouse. Notably, Mariman & Co. developed the Value Driven Management© platform for operating a multifamily investment portfolio and leveraging the demand for affordable housing. The result has been the creation of durable cash flows and risk-adjusted returns through the acquisition of low-income housing tax credit communities, with market value exceeding half a billion dollars. As Shawn would say, "We ventured down a road most people wouldn't have thought to take – and it's been quite a ride."

Gloria Soto:

I met Gloria in 2001. We married 12 years later in 2013. I had been unmarried for years and wanted someone in my life who could help me have a life outside my business. Her counsel and companionship have enriched my life. She is calm when I need reassurance, patient when I am not, and even-tempered. She is a kind "old soul," encouraging me to share my financial success with my Alma Mater, University of Portland. She thinks of me as a "young soul," a person who is young at heart. We have named my scholarship program, "The RUDY AND GLORIA MARIMAN FIRST GENERATION SCHOLARSHIP PROGRAM".

CHAPTER 10

REFLECTIONS, LESSONS LEARNED & RANDOM THOUGHTS

Every day, I set aside time for thinking.

Over the years, I have learned some lessons that have promulgated my success. I hope you find these observations useful in your own life and career.

Specialization.
When you specialize, you're focusing your efforts to maximize your success in one specialty, be it a career, sports, or volunteerism. Once you decide where you should focus your energy, concentrate your efforts accordingly. To be effective, I suggest you stick with your choice. Don't jump around in totally different directions or curriculums. In my case, I stayed with engineering for 7 years, then the land business for 10 years, and have been in the apartment business for more than 40 years. Elaborating further, I chose to specialize in apartments rather than strip centers, office, retail, or industrial real estate. Stay with your chosen vocation until you are successful, or determine another profession is a better fit. When I left the

engineering profession, I knew the land business was going to be my focus going forward. I ended up staying in the apartment business because I enjoyed the challenge and it seemed less risky than commercial real estate. Also, financing is more readily available.

Leverage.

Leverage in real estate is a key component in real estate investment. I used extreme leverage in the land business, never paying more than 10% down on any land purchase. When buying a parcel of land, I had monthly payments for 15 years. The key to the land business was to divide and sell at least two or more parcels creating a contractual monthly receivable payment greater than the purchase receivable, creating instant net cashflow. In the apartment business, I use leverage to breakeven or sometimes, I can afford a little negative cashflow for a period of time. Inflation or appreciation, efficient management, rent increases, and refinancing will in the long run payoff and provide income for life.

Write it Down.

As things pop in your mind, always, immediately write them down on a small tablet or electronic device. When you write things down, it clears up your mind for more creative thoughts and ideas. This habit is especially useful when a series of three or four ideas or thoughts appear all at once. This one habit of mine has made me a huge amount of money and more importantly keep my mind free to new ideas. It's impossible to remember all the good ideas you think about each day. I find it particularly helpful to write down ideas just before bed or even if I awake at night. It is generally, accepted business practice to write down the night before the things you want to accomplish the next day.

Buying Your First Home.
When you are contemplating buying your first home, hopefully, while in your twenties and are able to qualify for a home loan, I highly recommend considering buying a duplex, triplex, or maybe even a fourplex. Why? Collecting monthly rents from the tenants on the rental units help offset the mortgage payments, property taxes, upkeep, and you can depreciate a percentage of your investment. After a few years your tenants have contributed to reducing your mortgage debt, creating more equity. Later you will be able to afford a bigger house, and maybe even keep your income property too.

Control.
The two strongest words in the dictionary, *control and relative*. If you are in control you determine the outcome. Sooner or later, everything is relative. Basically, life's events fall into two categories: those that you can control (your choice), and those you cannot. Most events fortunately fall into the control category. Often, you might think something is outside of your ability to control, but upon closer examination you will discover the choices you made resulted in the events you experience. "You get what you ask for," sums up a person's ability to choose how your life unfolds.

For instance, being born in Berlin during WWII was not something I chose, nor was it my choice to immigrate to America. Once, I found myself living on my stepfather's farm, the choices I made shaped my life. I chose to obey my stepfather and worked on the farm as expected. I learned valuable life lessons on the farm. And I received wages for most of the work. As a result, I learned to save money. The habit of saving and keeping money is the first step to riches. Making the right choices is not always easy, nor can we foretell the consequences or rewards for all of our decisions. Every choice we make affects the choices we make thereafter.

In life, as you make choices, be sure to understand the consequences, good and bad. Feel comfortable to make decisions that benefit you even though your friends may disagree. Do not let other people deter you from making the right choices for you. Don't make excuses. Assuming you are making the right choices, take action and stick with your decisions. You may not know what vocation to choose when first starting out. That is OK. Begin your path in life, pursue your passion or best choice, overcoming challenges that may deter you. Have perseverance. Have stickability. Don't allow other people to discourage or dissuade you, especially as you begin to achieve success. Life is a series of choices, one leading to another, to another leading you to discover possibilities for achievement and success in your life. Once you find your path, stay in the groove and you will experience success.

Own vs Rent.

When it comes to major asset purchases, if it appreciates, such as, real estate, precious metals, or art, and collectables, such as classic cars or antiques, BUY IT. However, if it depreciates, rent it. Before you buy something, be sure you really want to own it. You may want to rent before you buy. Oftentimes, you may discover what you really wanted is no longer your cup of tea, and it might even become very embarrassing to own it. Buying something is permanent, renting is not. If possible, for big ticket items, rent it before making that buying decision.

Pilot's License.

As I reflect on my life, I realize I pretty much accomplished everything I set out to do. For instance, when I was 25 years old, I decided to get my private pilot's license. I reasoned, if I could fly prospective land buyers to the Antelope Valley to view their land, I could save several hours driving time to show land more effectively. I would pick them up at the Long Beach Airport. During the spring and summer months after work, I would fly prospects to see the land they were purchasing before the sun set. I know a lot of people who start their pilot's license training and never finish. Whatever you set out to do, finish it.

Accept Responsibility.
You can control your thinking; your thinking controls your behavior. Your behavior controls your results. If you're willing to learn instead of blame, life will go more smoothly for you. You can delegate authority, but never a responsibility.

Stay hungry. By the same token, stay humble. Contentment and complacency stifles creativity. If you are not careful, you will find yourself becoming content and complacent.

Reinvent yourself. Always be vigilant for the next opportunity. I am still actively seeking to refresh my viewpoints, looking for the next opportunity. Always be on the lookout.

Reinvent yourself, your education, attend seminars, and read not just for enjoyment, but for improvement. When you begin your career, you have at least 40 years to implement a financial, personal development, spiritual, social, and physical activity plan that is right for you. You can go through life being serious or silly. I prefer being serious about creating a productive life.

Have fun, laugh, but be serious about what you want to accomplish in life. Take responsibility for your life, no one else is going to. Don't be one of those people who spend money, they don't have to buy things they don't need to impress people they don't like.

My Three P's, Passion, Patience, Perseverance.
Always under promise, over deliver. Whether in your business or personal life, be patient, have perseverance and express passion. People will remember you when you express these character traits.

Ten Character Traits of a Positive Thinker. Optimism, Enthusiasm, Believe Integrity, Courage, Competence, Determination, Patience, Calmness, Focus.
When there is hope and faith in the future, there is power in the present. You must have something positive to hope for, otherwise, you have no expectation of receiving. We basically receive what we give to others in terms of friendship, respect, reverence, encouragement, gratitude, etc. When you're tough on yourself, life becomes easier. Don't make excuses. Perform a job to the best of your ability. If you don't have time to do it right the first time, how will you find time to do it over?

Taking Risks.
In 1980, I decided to make my first purchase of an apartment complex in another state, namely Dallas, Texas. I mentioned to my real estate broker, Bill Rietsch, I wanted to buy a large number of apartment units in a single purchase. Bill said it was not possible for me to do so in Southern California and suggested to look at out of state opportunities. I could buy apartments for one third the cost per unit in Texas. When making a decision, we do so with the best information available then take action.

I purchased a 388-unit apartment building in Dallas, on a leveraged purchase with only 10% down payment. I even doubled down and purchased an additional 94-unit building in Dallas. Both purchases were mistakes, I should never have purchased out of state property.

Eight years later, after losing approximately $20,000 per month, I finally was able to sell both buildings for about what I paid for them, not counting the negative cash flow. Looking back, the property I purchased was in the wrong area, the apartments were on a master meter system, and the buildings were in need of maintenance. Lastly, the economic recession of the early 1980's forced me to keep the property until the real estate market improved.

I survived this hardship by using much of my monthly revenue generated by my California investments. This experience was a major learning curve for me. I never again purchased property out of state. Today, I prefer to stay approximately a one-hour commute from any one property. When I make a mistake, I learn from that experience and do not repeat it again. The Dallas fiasco made me more conservative when investing for several years, which translated into slower growth for my business. Another lesson learned, do not let one mistake or misfortune knock you off track. Stick with your game plan, just don't repeat the same mistake.

Stay the Course.
Over the years, many-so-called outside investment opportunities have been presented to me. However, I never really veered from my game plan. As I mentioned earlier, stay in the groove dictated by your business plan (buy, hold, and manage southern California apartments) and stay focused. Salesmen tried to sell me various business opportunity ventures, they wanted me to buy stocks and bonds, or even buy a restaurant. I said NO to every one of these opportunities, stayed in the apartment house groove, and executed my game plan. For the past 40 plus years, I have not veered from my apartment business. Outside influences or temptations, come your way, but if what you are doing is working, stick by your guns and say "NO!"

NO!
Know when to say NO. Just that little word, "NO", oftentimes will make you money, save time, and keep you focused. Saying NO, makes you money because you don't lose money, waste time, or get side tracked. Very, very important.

Where to Live.
Remember, I came to southern California as a newly employed engineer. As a result, I bought my house in 1973. An unintended consequence is those of us who have been fortunate enough to invest (in my case, apartments) in Southern California property the past 40 years, have enjoyed wonderful appreciation, more so than probably most locations in the United States. Southern California is one of the top 10 areas experiencing steady appreciation, increasing property values 20-fold the past four decades. As a result, apartment buildings in California, in general, do not yield high percentage cap rate returns. Instead, investors enjoy high appreciation to offset low yields.

Deferred Property Maintenance.
Avoid deferred property maintenance at all costs. Over a period of many years I learned eventually to upgrade, rehab, & maintain my properties in pristine condition resulting in little or no deferred maintenance, less tenant turnover, and higher average rental income.

AFTERWORD

One thing should be clear after reading this book, Rudy Mariman is not your typical immigrant or businessman. His journey began in Berlin, Germany and ended in Newport Beach, California. How did this happen? Like many mothers in the world, Rudy's mother wanted a better life for her son. Leaving her homeland, her desire for a new start in life in America, gave Rudy an opportunity to learn life lessons, enabling him to become educated for a career and job in Southern California, where possibilities are waiting for those who seize the moment and dare to embrace new experiences.

Dear reader, you too can achieve success. Believe in yourself. Allow yourself to actively and deliberately create the life you truly want, instead of settling for the life the world presents to you. Rudy didn't enjoy his success over night, he persevered several decades observing successful people, saving money, willing to try something new, and once finding his passion, staying the course, and then finally enjoying the fruits of his success.

Rudy is not a conventional man. He says we should never follow the masses because the masses don't know who they are, where they are going, or what they really want. Raise your level of awareness of who you are and what is possible. Apply the success principles in this book in your own life. As you begin life's journey make a conscious effort to apply these principles in your life. All things are possible, if the motivation is strong enough. You too can be a financial success and become a multi-millionaire.

The Rudy & Gloria Mariman First Generation Scholarship Program is established to provide scholarships to first generation immigrant students attending the University of Portland. The program will be directed by my wife Gloria and the board of trustees, administered by my Alma Mater, University of Portland. OPB public broadcasting radio station in Portland, will receive some portion of my annual contribution.

If I have any advice for you, it is this: "Don't be afraid to take advantage of opportunities to better your circumstances". Some opportunities will come to your attention unexpectedly, sometimes in strange ways. Recognize an opportunity when you see it, act on it, pursue it, make it your chance to advance, or change your career. Remember, my chance meeting with Paul Connor, the land salesman. When Paul made an offer to me to find prospective land investors for a commission, I accepted. We both recognized a mutually beneficial opportunity. I helped him sell land, and he in turn educated me how the land business works.

We have heard that there are two kinds of people out there. <u>Dreamers:</u> they never give up on life; and <u>Realists:</u> they work diligently. And while I, for a long time, agreed with this, I have come to realize there is a third category of people: <u>The Realistic Dreamer.</u> Nobody is 100% one way or the other, but they may lean more in one direction. It's a spectrum, and the good news is that **you** can shift the paradigm, so **you**'re a little more balanced. Remember that being a **doer** isn't necessarily better than being a **dreamer**. Why not be a **realistic dreamer**, in other words, allow your dreams to become true with a plan of action. Keep your dreams alive. Understand to achieve anything, requires faith and belief in yourself, vision, hard work, determination, and dedication. Remember you can achieve anything that you set your mind to. Give yourself a command and follow it.

ACKNOWLEDGEMENTS

The idea for this book came about in a conversation I had with Craig Batley how to best communicate with the recipients of scholarships provided by the Rudy & Gloria Mariman First Generation Scholarship Program. Craig suggested I write a book, telling my own story of immigrating to America from Germany in the early 1950's. We agreed to collaborate to make this book possible. Craig recorded many conversations of me recollecting highlights of my life beginning in Berlin, Germany from early childhood in the early 1940's to arriving in Oregon at age 14. I have included life experiences that may be of interest to young first-generation immigrants just entering the freshman class of the University of Portland. We attempted to share events that others may have experienced. You may find some of my experiences, similar to your own. Hopefully, the events I share may provide guide posts for those of you who desire to excel in their career or even start their own entrepreneurial business.

Also, I want to extend a debt of gratitude to those individuals who contributed to my life in so many ways as a young person right up to today. In many ways this book was made possible because of the contribution each of these people made in my life. I would like to extend a debt of gratitude to everyone listed below who changed my life for the better, making this book possible.

Grandfather (Opa): Albert Wiedemann
He played a pivotal part in our small family, everything revolved around him. He was the back bone of our family. I owe everything to my grandfather, since he coaxed my mom to immigrate to America.

Mom:
My mom was most instrumental person in my life. Her courage to take the two of us to the German countryside and then later immigrate to America changed both of our lives beyond measure.

George, My Stepfather:
Very fair but firm. He was my boss. I worked for George during the summers and weekends from 1955 to 1962. Initially, he paid me the going pay rate starting at 50 cents per hour and as my work skills improved I eventually earned $1.75 per hour. I developed a work ethic, while living and working on George's farm.

Paul Connor:
Most charismatic guy I ever met. Offered me a part-time job as his "bird dog", referring him fellow engineers to buy land in the Antelope Valley. Within a year, I made more money part-time with him than full-time as an engineer. Knowing Paul put me in the land business. Initially he used me for his benefit; but after about two years, I started my own bird dog team and sold land I purchased in order to resale land to investors. The land business allowed me to make the transition from engineering to owning and managing apartments.

Dick Farley:
He and two partners ran a land company bussing people up to Antelope Valley from Orange County every weekend on two Greyhound

buses. They had up to 100 part-time salesmen. I learned a great deal from him about the land business, especially how to think "outside the box".

Craig Batley:
He called potential land investors, making appointments for me to sell land I owned in Antelope Valley. He was instrumental in getting me interested in diversifying my business by investing in buying apartments. Since 1973, over the years he has helped me organize and streamline my business. Finally, it was Craig who suggested I write a book to present to all Rudy & Gloria Mariman First Generation Immigrant Scholarship Program recipients.

Bill Rietsch:
My acquisition broker from 1975 to 1995.

Peter Hauser:
My acquisition broker from 1995 to present.

Rich & Rick Hoegler:
Rich visited one of my properties 14 years ago and made me realize I was not maintaining my properties to maximize long term ownership. He was right. I hired his company, Pan American Properties, Inc. to completely rehab all my properties from 2004 to 2008. His son, Rick, did a terrific job. This experience completely changed my investment philosophy, and now all my properties are in pristine condition.

Sandy Weston:
Sandy has worked for Mariman & Co. for over 15 years, immeasurably helping me make the transition from an old-style apartment

portfolio manager to a highly sophisticated, cloud-based management team. Every CEO needs a Sandy, whose job title is Corporate Office Manager.

Shawn Boyd:

Shawn is the COO & CFO and all-around key employee of Mariman & Company. Shawn has positioned Mariman & Co. to become one of California's most prolific direct investors in affordable housing. Notably Shawn engineered the Value Driven Management© platform system for operating a multifamily investment portfolio and leveraging the demand for affordable housing.

Gloria Soto:

Gloria is my wife and life partner. She has made me a better man. Being a giving person, she encouraged me to become a benefactor of the University of Portland. Gloria is the love of my life.

EPILOGUE

At this stage in my life, I am basically retired. I have no day-to-day job. I enjoy going to the office pretty much every day around 11:00AM, for a couple hours, to analyze potential apartment investment opportunities. I review the monthly financials and tracking reports prepared by my accountant and CFO. I have delegated all day-to-day responsibility to my COO & CFO. I generally leave for lunch around 1:00PM, and seldom come back to the office until the following day. Remember, I have worked for 50 years to reach the level of success enjoyed by Mariman & Company. However, if it is possible for an immigrant teenager from Berlin Germany, who spoke nothing but broken English when he settled in Estacada, Oregon to eventually experience business success, then it is possible for you too. Become a realistic dreamer.

APPENDIX

RUDYISMS

*Guiding Principles and Words of Wisdom
I've Tried to Live By and Adhere To.*

Don't let others derail you—stay the course. Many opportunities came my way to alter my focus—I never went for it. Never veered from my main focus at the time. Outside influences come your way—stick to your guns, as they say.

Sometimes you make money by saying no. Stay focused.

Taking risks is the only way to consistently achieve above average returns in life as well as with an investment.

Be sure you get your thought across. Make sure you ask if you are well understood; repeat your thought if you have to; don't take their understanding for granted.

Be a good listener, gather up information pertaining to your subject as much as possible. Then, make up your own mind.

Reputation is your most important asset.

I thrive on inspiring and challenging people, sometimes testing them at the same time.

I learned from early on "Economic Success Equals Freedom."

Really listening is at the heart of any negotiation and understanding what is truly important to the other person is of paramount importance.

In business, know when to say no, often times you make money by saying no.

Silly vs. Serious. Save and be serious the first half of your life, so you can enjoy the second half.

As things pop in your mind, always write them down, consequently clears up your mind, afterward you'll be glad you did. Impossible to remember more than three items at a time.

Two strongest words in the dictionary are "control" and "relative.

With control you have everything; sooner or later everything is relative.

Make the most out of what you already have; improve upon it before replacing it.

What goes up in value, own; what goes down in value, rent.

Before purchasing big ticket items, always rent first before owning; it may turn out you don't want to own it.

Don't emphasize the problem so much—emphasize the solution.

Look at yourself first when things go wrong.

The most stressful condition a person can face is not having something to believe in.

You can control your thinking. Your thinking can control your behavior.

Your behavior controls your results.

If you are willing to learn instead of blame, life will go more smoothly.

Two Doors in Life - Security and Freedom. If you choose the door marked security, you lose both.

Awareness is the first step to progress.

Without passion, you don't have energy. Without energy, you have nothing.

You can delegate authority—but never responsibility.

Keep financially negative people out of your lives—surround yourselves with like-minded people who challenge and support you.

Our friends are part of our environment.

Stay hungry—stay humble.
Contentment and complacency stifles creativity.
We constantly need to reinvent ourselves.

Perfectionist vs Pessimist vs Realist: don't be either one, be a blend.

The new generation will ask:
Why are we not seeking alternative energy sources?
Why not focus on reducing global warming?
Why is there poverty?
Why are there different tax laws for different people?
Why don't we teach kids about money in school?
I know I'm still overpaying, but I know you'll do a great job.
Don't let me down.
A compliment from me has special meaning.

Here is to our town:

1. Where people spend money they don't have.
2. To buy things they don't need.
3. To impress people they don't like.

Never give up on your vision—especially when you believe in it, with passion and conviction come success.

Why R.E. is an **IDEAL** Investment	5 Kinds of Leverage
Income	OPM-other people's money
Deduction	OPE-other people's experience
Equity	OPI-other people's ideas
Appreciation	OPT-other people's time
Leverage	OPW-other people's work

My 3 P's: Passion   Patience   Perseverance
Under Promise ~ Over Deliver

Ten Traits of a Positive Thinker

1. Optimism
2. Enthusiasm
3. Belief
4. Integrity
5. Courage
6. Confidence
7. Determination
8. Patience
9. Calmness
10. Focus

If there is Hope and Faith in the future, there is Power in the present.

When you are tough on yourself, life becomes easier.

It's easier to explain price once, then it is to apologize for quality forever.

Be more than what you portray to be.

We buy properties not to milk them, but to build them.

It is far better to buy a great property at a fair price than to buy a fair property at a great price.

It's not who you know, but "Whom you seek to know" that benefits you the most.

Understand first before trying to be understood, ask questions. Too many people don't ask questions and don't think without specific questions. If you don't ask questions, how can you expect specific answers?

Real estate is an IDEAL investment

 I ncome
 D epreciation
 E quity buildup
 A ppreciation
 L everage

You have not because you ask not.

People are so ready to blame others instead of taking responsibility for their actions.

Remember as you go through life, some things you want to own, and a lot you want to rent.

Never take advice from anyone who doesn't have what you want.

We live in a world where there is much said, but little done.

Remember you can lose your money and make more, but you can never replace your time.

If you ever earn anything in this world, you must get it on your own.

Never accept a map from someone who hasn't been where you want to go.

Man is rich in proportion to the number of things he can accomplish.

Some things you want to own, and a lot you want to rent.

"Fake it until you make it" used to be a blatant insult to people, just might be sound business strategy today.

OTHERS' FAVORITE QUOTES

Inflation is an enemy of cash. It spends so easy and is so hard to save.

The easiest way to separate you from your money is for you to invest in things that depreciate over time. The second easiest way to is to give your money to someone else to invest.

The best way to invest your money is to buy things that go up in value or appreciate. Things like a home or rental income property, a business, good stocks and keep them. The keeping is where the money is made in most cases.

In acquiring properties, it is best to have a real estate agent that represents you. On creative financing or market conditions, your realtor is of great help. But don't expect them to buy into your investment philosophy. Just as most bankers never get rich; so most real estate agents just work for a living. Remember knowledge and understanding of ways to buy rental property can be learned from your realtor.

Remember the selling realtor only makes money on what he sells. He will always tell you that every listing he has for sale is a good deal.

You need a realtor that you are comfortable with. The same way you need a doctor, lawyer, insurance agent, accountant, or banker. A person you can befriend, ask questions, discuss deals, strategies, and know his recommendation to buy is based on honest research. To find such a broker may take time, but it is time well spent.

Remember, life is a series of corrections. When you are in business these corrections are an absolute necessity for survival. Many businesses fail because the owner would not face the truth about his business or his ability, or maybe pride prevents him from asking for help. As a business man you are the servant of all your customers (in the rental business that means tenants). There is no room for pride or arrogance.

Truth shows you your weaknesses and teaches you to delegate to others regarding things where you are not well versed. Recognize your own strengths and weaknesses.

Saving money is the beginning of all investing. However, borrowing money (leveraging) is the only way to build wealth in real estate.

F – Follow
O – One
C – Course
U – Until
S – Successful

EXHIBITS

MISSILE & SPACE SYSTEMS DIVISION
DOUGLAS AIRCRAFT COMPANY, INC.
SANTA MONICA CALIFORNIA

March 16, 1962

Mr. Rudy A. Mariman
3100 S. E. McLaughlin
Portland 2, Oregon

Dear Mr. Mariman:

We are pleased to offer you a position at our Missile and Space Systems Division as an Associate Production Design Engineer in the Production Liaison Section at a beginning salary of $555.00 Per Month.

Your assignment will be varied and general within the function of the Section as described in the enclosed sheets from our Organization Manual. As you become acquainted with the Company practices and procedures, you will be given specialized technical responsibilities in keeping with your interests and existing opportunity.

Our offer includes personal travel, per diem and moving allowances, as outlined in the enclosed employment agreement. If you accept, we ask that you and your physician complete the enclosed physical examination form and a chest X-ray, in order to be reasonably assured of passing our medical requirements. Please forward the form and X-ray, apart from any correspondence, to our Medical Director, Department A-360. Upon receipt of one signed copy of the employment agreement, receipt and approval of your preliminary physical examination form, and approximately one month prior to your departure, we will forward your transportation allowance. Allow at least two weeks for processing the preliminary physical examination. Shortly after return of the signed agreement, you will be contacted by a specific van company in your area who is the agent for the long distance van company which will arrange final delivery for your household goods.

Douglas is sending you a one week subscription to the Santa Monica Evening Outlook, a local newspaper, which will help to determine the cost and availability of housing, the general cost of living and some of the activities in this vicinity. We are also sending you the next four issues of our Company newspaper, Airview News.

We look forward to your joining this organization and to receiving your acceptance within the next sixty days.

Very truly yours,

MISSILE AND SPACE SYSTEMS DIVISION
Douglas Aircraft Company, Inc.

E. T. Kennedy
Engineering Personnel Manager
Missile Systems

ETK/ sw
Encls.

Rudy's First Job Hiring Letter from Douglas.

Outstanding Job Performance Recognition Letter.

NORTH AMERICAN AVIATION, INC. SPACE and INFORMATION SYSTEMS DIVISION

APOLLO PRIDE IN ENGINEERING

North American Aviation and the Apollo Team
take great pride in recognizing

RUDY A. MARIMAN

and his associates of

LC-39 FACILITIES

for achieving the highest performance score
of the Apollo Engineering Department in the measured
excellence of technical, schedule, and budgetary
management in engineering the
GSE PATCHING, CABLING AND FACILITIES
ICD'S FOR SPACECRAFT 017 & 020
JULY - SEPTEMBER 1966

G. W. Jeffs
Asst. Program Manager
Apollo Chief Program Engineer

Outstanding Job Performance Recognition Letter.

First Commission Check from Paul Connor.

TO MY MOM OR "MOMSY" AS I LOVINGLY CALLED YOU.

THANKS MOMSY...

FOR YOUR COURAGE AND CHARM, YOUR WIT THAT WOULD MAKE ME LAUGH WHEN I GOT TOO SERIOUS.

FOR COMFORTING ME WHEN I WAS AFRAID OR SICK.

FOR STICKING UP FOR ME EVEN IF I WAS WRONG.

FOR HAVING THE STRENGTH TO BRING ME TO AMERICA AND ALLOWING ME THE OPPORTUNITY TO BE EDUCATED HERE AND TO EXCEL IN LIFE WHICH ALL HAS BECOME ...BECAUSE OF YOU!

SO REST IN PEACE BELOVED MOTHER ON THIS BEAUTIFUL SUNNY AUTUMN DAY. AND, THANK YOU FOR ALL THE LOVE AND SACRIFICES THAT YOU MADE FOR ME AND THE MOMENTS OF LAUGHTER AND JOY HAT YOU BROUGHT TO MANY PEOPLES' LIVES THAT YOU TOUCHED IF ONLY FOR A BRIEF MOMENT.

LOVE, RUDY

Rudy's Letter to Heidi Mariman at her Memorial.

Rudy Mariman at the Mariman & Co. corporate offices in 2018.

www.ingramcontent.com/pod-product-compliance
Lightning Source LLC
Chambersburg PA
CBHW052201110526
44591CB00012B/2030